Nature's Children

SEALS

Merebeth Switzer

GROLIER
EDUCATIONAL

FACTS IN BRIEF

Classification of North American earless seals

Class: *Mammalia* (mammals)

Order: *Carnivora* (meat-eating mammals)

Family: *Phocidae* (seal family)

Genus and species: 13 genera and 18 species exist around the world. The most common in North America are—Harbor Seal, Harp Seal, Ringed Seal, Bearded Seal, Gray Seal, Hooded Seal, Northern Elephant Seal.

World Distribution. Seals are found throughout the polar regions, and as far south as California and New York in North America, Wales in Europe and Japan in Asia.

Habitat. Usually live where ocean water meets land or solid ice; may move into fresh water; some seals migrate in search of food.

Distinctive Physical Characteristics. Have no external ears, simply openings on side of head; rear flippers cannot be turned forward; coarse stiff coat with no underfur.

Diet. Mainly fish but also eat various other sea animals.

Published originally as
"Getting to Know . . . Nature's Children."

This series is approved and recommended by the Federation of Ontario Naturalists.

This library reinforced edition is available exclusively from:

GROLIER
EDUCATIONAL

Sherman Turnpike, Danbury, Connecticut 06816

Contents

What barks like a dog, has whiskers like a cat and swims like a fish? If you guessed a seal, congratulations! Seals have an unusual combination of features that equip them for life on land as well as in the water. They are one of the few animals that are at home in both worlds.

When people think about seals they often picture performing seals. But most of the animals that perform in zoos and marine parks are not seals, they are Sea Lions.

The seal, nonetheless, is a superb swimmer. It can do a flashy combination of spins, twirls and somersaults then disappear below the surface in an amazing speed dive.

On land, seals are not as graceful as they are in water. But they seem to enjoy sunbathing and talking to friends, much like vacationers at a beach.

Harbor Seals, like all of us, enjoy relaxing on sandy beaches.

Inquisitive Pups

The sleek, smooth body of the pudgy young seal skims through the water of the harbor. Suddenly it stops and pops its head up to check its surroundings. Its large brown eyes focus on a sailboat gliding quietly by. Overcome by curiosity it watches, bobbing closer to this strange object. Suddenly a flapping sail unfurls. The pup dives deep into the water. Even though it is curious, it will leave this giant sea monster alone!

The young seal's natural curiosity disappears as it grows up and becomes more cautious about the world around it. This is important. In order to survive the pup must learn to be wary.

Is the coast clear? (Gray Seal pup)

Fin-Footed Families

There are many different kinds of seals. They all belong to a group of animals called pinnipeds, which means "fin-footed." You have only to look at their large, flipper-like feet to know why scientists have given them this name. Flippers are much more useful than ordinary feet when you spend as much time in the water as pinnipeds do.

Eared seal

The pinniped group is made up of three families—walruses, eared seals (which include Sea Lions and fur seals) and earless seals, often called true seals. The earless seal family is the biggest and most widespread of the three pinniped families. There are 18 kinds of earless seals and about half of them are found in North America.

Earless seal

Only the Fur Seal has the soft, thick underfur which many people associate with seals, but it is not actually a true or earless seal. Like Sea Lions, it belongs to the eared seal family.

Seal front flipper

Sea Lion front flipper

Opposite page:

When a seal dives, flaps close over its ear openings. (Harbor Seal)

Seal or Sea Lion?

It is not surprising that people sometimes get Seals and Sea Lions confused. But if you look closely, you will spot some differences.

First look at their ears. Sea Lions have ears that are easy to see. No wonder they belong to the group called "eared" seals. Although seals have ears too, their ears are only tiny openings on the sides of their heads. They do not have ear flaps as Sea Lions do.

All Seals and Sea Lions are beautifully streamlined for life in the water, but their hind legs are quite different. As a result, they swim and move on the land in different ways. Sea Lions can walk and even run on land because they can stand on their hind feet. In the water they "row" with their large front flippers and steer with their back feet. Seals use their hind legs as a huge fin to do most of the swimming work.

On land, a seal's hind legs are of little use. Instead of walking, it wriggles along like an overgrown caterpillar.

Creature of Two Worlds

The seal is a creature of two worlds—water and land. It moves with grace and ease through water as it searches for food. Unlike most aquatic animals, it can move from salt water to fresh water if the need arises.

But the seal is a mammal. It needs to breathe air and it must come ashore to mate, to bear its young and to rest.

From the ice floes of the Arctic to the rocky shores of Newfoundland and the sandy beaches of California, the seal lives in areas where water meets land or solid ice.

In North America, seals may be found as far south as New York on the Atlantic Coast and all the way down to California and Mexico on the Pacific Coast.

This Harp Seal pup is quite at home in its frozen world of ice and snow.

Watery Wonder

A seal is wonderfully suited to its watery existence. Its sleek, torpedo-shaped body glides easily through the water and helps make it a first class swimmer.

Seals are remarkable in their ability to remain underwater for long periods of time. Many can stay underwater for about 20 minutes. How do they manage?

Before a seal dives, it breathes out all the air in its body. With no air in its lungs, diving is easier and safer. But the seal's heart and brain, like yours, need oxygen. And like you, the seal can only get oxygen from air. Unlike you, however, the seal can make especially efficient use of the oxygen dissolved in its blood when it is underwater. Until it comes to the surface again to breathe, most of this oxygen goes to its most important body parts—the heart and brain.

World class swimmer. (Harbor Seal)

Diving Champs

Scuba divers must envy seals. Without special equipment, human divers can only go to a depth of 45 metres (150 feet). Diving any deeper is dangerous. But many seals can dive twice as deep as a human. And some, such as the Elephant Seal, can reach depths of about 300 metres (1000 feet).

Your heart beats about 72 times a minute. A seal's heart normally beats much faster, about 150 times per minute. But when the seal dives, its heart rate drops to 60 beats per minute. On very deep or long dives, it may drop as low as 10 to 20 beats per minute. By slowing its heart down in this way, the seal can make its oxygen supply last longer.

Taking a breather. (Harbor Seal)

Beautiful, Beautiful Brown Eyes

The seal's large brown eyes have special features to help it to see underwater. Because it can be very dark deep down in the ocean, the pupils of the seal's eyes open extra wide to let in more light. Out of the water, in bright sunlight, the pupils shrink to a tiny slit.

If you have ever swum in the ocean, you probably know that if you try to keep your eyes open, the salt water will make them sting after a while. Seals do not have this problem. They have an extra, transparent eyelid that they can pull over their eyes to protect them when they are underwater.

Finally, seals do a lot of crying—but not because they are sad. The seal cannot control the tears that flow from its eyes. Just as your eyes water to wash away a speck of dust, the seal's tears flow freely to wash away anything that might irritate its eyes.

Harp Seal

Sizing up Seals

Most types of seals range between one and two metres (3-6 feet) in length and weigh 90 to 225 kilograms (200 to 500 pounds). But male Northern Elephant Seals can grow to more than 6 metres (20 feet) long and weigh as much as 3600 kilograms (8000 pounds). That's longer than most people's living rooms and heavier than two cars! In fact, the Elephant Seal is one of the largest animals in the world.

As is the case with many animals, the males, or bulls, are often much bigger than the females, or cows.

It's no mystery how the large Northern Elephant Seal got its name.

A Blanket of Blubber

Imagine hopping into a bathtub full of cold water and blocks of ice. Brrr! You would feel like a human icicle seconds after you plunged in! But not seals. Seals can spend long periods of time swimming in freezing water that is often part ice and part water. They are protected by a thick layer of body fat, called blubber, under their skin. A seal's blubber may be up to 15 centimetres (6 inches) thick. This thick blanket of blubber acts as insulation, keeping the seal's body heat in, and the cold out.

Blubber also helps to smooth out the seal's body shape, making it even more streamlined for swimming. And, because it is light, blubber helps keep the seal afloat, so that it does not have to work as hard when swimming.

Seals find their blubber very useful in another way, too. When necessary, they can go weeks without eating, drawing the energy they need from their blubber.

Opposite page:

"Come on in—the water's fine!" (Gray Seal)

22

Air-Conditioning Flippers

Believe it or not a seal is kept so warm by its layer of blubber that it sometimes gets overheated. Since the seal cannot take off its blubber blanket when it gets hot, it has come up with another way to cool off. It gets rid of extra heat through its flippers.

The seal's flippers are not covered with blubber. Instead they are crisscrossed with blood vessels. When the seal gets too warm, it can pump large amounts of blood through its flippers. There the blood is cooled by the surrounding air or water. The cooled blood returns to the body and soon the seal's temperature has returned to normal.

Tell-Tale Teeth

The teeth and claws of seals are made up of layers, like tree rings. A new layer is added every year. By counting the layers, scientists can tell a seal's age. Some seals live up to 40 or more years in the wild.

The seal has few natural enemies, except the Polar Bear and Killer Whale. Arctic Foxes and sharks also prey on seals.

Young seals are particularly vulnerable especially during their first weeks of life. A Golden Eagle, walrus or other large predator considers a baby seal an easy meal.

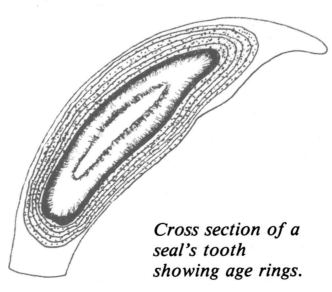

Cross section of a seal's tooth showing age rings.

Who Are You?

To us, most seals look a lot alike. It is difficult to tell one from another. Seals seem to have the same problem. On a crowded beach they do not seem to be able to tell their own babies from other babies or friends from strangers just by looking.

Instead, they use smell and sound to help them identify other seals. Most seals have a keen sense of smell. The mother seal uses this to recognize her own baby. This is very important if she is in a large group with other seals and their young.

Seals also use a wide range of calls to find a friend in a crowd. These "Who are you?" calls vary with the type of seal. Some make funny grunts and squeaks while others make dog-like barks.

Hooded Seal

Seals—Alone and Together

When you think of seals, you may think of large groups of them clustered together on a beach. Or you may think of a few seals playing together.

Many seals do live in groups. Some seals gather when ashore but disperse when they return to the water to feed. Others, such as the Harp Seal, spend all their time in groups. During mating and traveling, Harp Seal herds may number thousands of animals.

But other kinds of seals live alone. The Ringed Seal, in particular, spends nearly all of its time on its own. The mother gives birth to one baby in a secluded den she digs under the snow or in a natural hollow in the ice. Mother and baby stay together for about two months. Except for this time, however, and a brief time spent with a mate, the Ringed Seal remains alone.

Harbor Seals

Seal-Time Meal-Time

Since seals search for food in the water, you can probably guess one of their favorite foods. That's right—fish.

But seals eat other foods as well. Harbor Seals search in tidepools for small sea creatures left behind by the outgoing tide. The ocean-roaming Harp Seal eats small fish such as herring and capelin and masses of tiny, shrimp-like animals called krill.

Many seals prefer to eat bottom-living animals such as crabs, clams, whelks, shrimp, snails and octopuses. In fact, the Bearded Seal has special whiskers like the walrus's to help it search for tasty treats on the dark ocean bottom. Scientists think that it rakes up the bottom with its front claws and then uses its whiskers to sift through the debris. When the Bearded Seal finds a yummy whelk or succulent clam it uses it strong jaws and teeth to crush the shell to get at the food. Since it does not need the shell in its diet, it spits out the broken pieces.

Opposite page:

A seal's whiskers are sensitive feelers that help it find food in the murky ocean depths. (Harbor Seal)

Long Journeys

You probably know that many birds migrate, traveling south at about the same time every fall, then north again in the spring. But did you know that some seals do the same thing? When winter comes, seals that live in large groups in Arctic waters must migrate to find food. Some of them may travel hundreds of kilometres.

The Harp Seal is probably the best known migrator. In summer, when northern waters teem with small fish and tiny marine animals, Harp Seals live and feed in the water at the edge of the Arctic pack ice. In fall, as the ice begins to spread southward over their feeding grounds, the seals move southward ahead of it. Then in spring they follow the melting edge northward again.

Not all kinds of seals migrate. Those that live alone or in small groups have little need to make these long seasonal journeys in search of food.

Harp Seal and pup.

Birth Time

Baby seals may be born at different times of year, depending on the type of seal and where its home is. Most seal mothers, however, give birth in late winter. They haul themselves out onto the ice or onto land to have their babies.

Some cows gather in large groups to have their babies, others give birth alone. In either case, the bulls usually stay away from the females at this time. They may form bachelor groups or go off by themselves. They do not help care for the babies when they are born.

With a pup this young, mom is probably not far away.(Harbor Seal)

Meet the Baby

The seal babies, or pups, are quite small compared to their mothers. Ringed Seal babies may weigh as little as four and a half kilograms (10 pounds), while Bearded Seal pups may weigh as much as 36 kilograms (80 pounds).

Most seals that are born on ice or snow have a soft woolly white coat. This is very important for it will keep them warm until their bodies have a chance to build up a layer of blubber. A white coat also helps the pup blend into its snowy home, so that it is not easily spotted by predators.

Seals that are born on cliffs or sandy beaches are usually a dark brown or mottled color. This helps them blend in with the rocky or sandy beaches on which they spend the first weeks of their life.

A Harbor Seal's pup is usually born with a coat very much like that of its mother.

A Caring Mother

Baby seals begin to feed on their mother's milk minutes after they are born. Some nurse in the water, others on land or on ice floes. The milk is so rich that it looks just like soft creamy butter.

Most baby seals do not spend a long time with their mother, but while they do, they are well cared for. The mother stays near her baby, ready for its almost constant demands to nurse. If she does leave for any reason, she is seldom gone for long.

Getting to know each other. (Harbor Seal mother and pup)

38

Swimming Lessons

Seals are natural swimmers, but this does not mean that they jump right into the water. This strange new wetness requires a close checking before the first plunge. The curious pup sidles up to the water's edge and after a sniff and sidelong glance it dumps its body in. The flustered baby bobs in the water unsure of its new surroundings. Soon, though, it will be swimming with the same ease and grace as its parents. When it needs a rest a tired pup may hitch a ride on its mother's shoulders.

Hooded Seal pups are called bluebacks because of their blue-tinged fur.

A Hasty Departure

Some pups have two months or more of their mother's care, but many are left to fend for themselves when they are about two weeks old. These pups are well prepared for life on their own, however. They are already at home in the water, and most have grown-up teeth for feeding. In other words, they have all the tools they need to survive. They simply need to learn how to use them. And until they do learn to catch their own food, they can live off their blubber.

There are reasons for the mother seal's rather hasty departure. If she is to have another baby next year, she has to seek out a male to mate with. Also, the cow seal has not eaten since giving birth. In supplying milk for her baby, she has already used up a great deal of her body fat. If she is to survive to mate, she must stop nursing her young.

Opposite page:

When a male Hooded Seal inflates the elastic skin over its nose into a "hood", it is warning intruders to stay away.

Mating Time

Mating usually takes place a few weeks after the cows have left their pups. At this time the cows and bulls seek each other out. Some bulls will put on spectacular swimming displays to impress a female, and often two bulls will fight each other to determine who will father the young.

Among some types of seals, a powerful bull may set up a harem of several cows. He will mate with the cows in his harem and protect them from the advances of other males. At first he will probably just try to discourage an intruding male by lowering his head and hissing. If that does not work, he will fight. Usually the intruder gives up before anyone is seriously hurt.

During the mating season some male seals give off a powerful musky odor. As unappealing as this smells to us, it works to attract female seals.

Opposite page:

Within two to three weeks after birth the long cream-colored coat of this Gray Seal pup will be shed, and replaced with a much darker coat similar to that of its parents.

New Coats for Old

After the adult seals mate, they shed their coats. By this time their old coats are ragged and shaggy. They have been worn away in many places over the past year. In some cases the coat sheds in large pieces, sometimes taking old, dead outer skin with it.

While they are molting, the seals rest and remain on land. They do not eat. Instead, they live off their stores of blubber. Within a few weeks, the bulls and cows have grown new coats of coarse fur.

It is now time to return to the ocean for their first meal in a long time. The seals head out in search of food. Most will live out in the ocean until next spring when they will again haul themselves out onto the land or ice where the next generation of pups will be born.

Words to Know

Bull Male seal.

Cow Female seal.

Ice Floes Large floating pieces of flat ice.

Lungs The part of the body that takes oxygen from the air and makes it available to the rest of the body.

Mating Coming together to produce young.

Migration Traveling at regular times of the year in search of food or a place to give birth.

Molt To shed a coat of fur and grow another.

Nurse To drink milk from a mother's body.

Oxygen The part of the air that is used by the body.

Pinnipeds A group of animals whose legs are specially shaped as flippers. Seals, Sea Lions and walruses are pinnipeds.

Predator Animal that hunts other animals for food.

Pup Young seal.

Pupil The inner circle of the eye, which opens and closes to take in light.

Tidepool A pool of water left on the shore when the tide goes out.

INDEX

Cover Photo: Kennon Cooke
Photo Credits: Harold V. Green (Valan Photos), page 4; Val and Alan Wilkinson (Valan Photos), pages 7, 34; Stephen J. Krasemann (Valan Photos), pages 8, 37; Kennon Cooke (Valan Photos), page 11; Fred Bruemmer, pages 12, 20, 23, 33, 39, 43; Michel Bourque (Valan Photos), page 15; François Lepine (Valan Photos), page 16; Norman Lightfoot (Eco-Art Productions), page 19; W. Hoek (Valan Photos), page 26; Wamboldt-Waterfield (Miller Services), page 29; Esther Schmidt (Valan Photos), page 30; Valan Photos, page 40; Anthony J. Bond (Valan Photos), page 44.

Printed and Bound in Italy by Lego SpA